Tales of the Zodiac

Tales of the Zodiac

A Poetic Journey Through the Cosmos

By
Malika Semper

Two Suns Publishing

Copyright © 2025 Malika Semper

All rights reserved. No part of this publication may be reproduced, distributed, or transmitted in any form or by any means, including photocopying, recording, digital scanning, or other electronic or mechanical methods, without the prior written permission of the publisher, except in the case of brief quotations embodied in critical reviews and certain other noncommercial uses permitted by copyright law.

Published 2025
Hardcover ISBN: 979-8-9987402-0-6
Ebook ISBN: 979-8-9987402-1-3

Tale Art by Caitlyn Grabenstein. Instagram: @cult.class
Book design by Stacey Aaronson. www.thebookdoctorisincom

Published by:
Two Suns Publishing

For inquiries, please address:
support@malikasemperastrology.com

Printed in the United States of America

NO AI TRAINING: Without in any way limiting the author's [and publisher's] exclusive rights under copyright, any use of this publication to "train" generative artificial intelligence (AI) technologies to generate text is expressly prohibited. The author reserves all rights to license uses of this work for generative AI training and development of machine learning language models.

For Jonah & Elia,
both my suns who have taught me the most about the archetypes.

CONTENTS

Foreword by Debra Silverman ... i
Introduction 1

An Aries Tale 11
A Taurus Tale 15
A Gemini Tale 19
A Cancer Tale 23
A Leo Tale 27
A Virgo Tale 31
A Libra Tale 35
A Scorpio Tale 39
A Sagittarius Tale 43
A Capricorn Tale 47
An Aquarius Tale 51
A Pisces Tale 55

Gratitude 59
About the Author 63

Foreword

Some people are given the gift to hear the whispers from the voices of those who sing poetry in our dreams. Some souls come down here to feel what we cannot feel because they are our doorways, our teachers. Some beings have the gift of words as they stream together pearls that become the crumbs in the story of Hansel and Gretel that take us home.

Malika is such a poet/writer/listener/astrologer. The gifts she carries melt our hearts open. Our minds touch our souls and remind us of the beauty of the astrological mythology that is translated by the ones who have the gift—and Malika has that gift. I follow her and her words into a new version of the signs that lift me up and remind me of beauty.

I think of myself as a poet, but I don't have Neptune on my sun like she does. I am not the whimsical, dreamy writer who is awakened in the nighttime within an assignment to write about the twelve astrological signs with words that soothe; rather, I am a poet who spends her days in the earthbound world to maintain my business and share my knowledge through a school.

It's a small detail that Malika is one of my favorite people on Earth, one I'm lucky enough to call sister/friend. She has surpassed my expectations with the gift of her words and in bringing astrology into my heart.

Enjoy this book and let your poet be ignited as you, too, aspire to be a channel for the whispers of those voices that live beyond this world.

—Debra Silverman
Founder of Applied Astrology

INTRODUCTION

Once upon a time, beneath a full Scorpio moon, Aries whispered in my ear. I turned on the light to cast away the 2 a.m. shadows, fumbling for my notebook on my nightstand. Bleary-eyed, I jotted down the words Aries was telling me. Writing in the stillness of the night made the words feel more magical, and so for the next two hours, I acquiesced to Aries, scribbling passionately, following his lead. *And so began the journey through the tales.*

I followed the stars down to Earth. My double-Libra mother was baking Zimtsterne (a German Christmas cookie, translated to "Cinnamon Stars") when she went into labor with me. There was a nip to the air that cold December night in Frankfurt as I came into the world. The sky was dark and moody, and the balsamic Sagittarius moon was a tiny sliver in the sky.

As a little girl, you'd find me barefoot with messy hair, a girl who loved her grandmother. I grew up rich in magic, creating a world of make-believe around me, feeling the unseen.

At four years old, we boarded a plane, my parents and I, and came to live in the States. I remember sitting in the trees and building forts in the California vineyards, which grew all around me. The large leaves created a halo of comfort acting as my roof and walls, forever imprinting the soft shade of green in me as safe—a color where imagination comes to life.

My mother read *Brothers Grimm Fairy Tales* to me as I drifted to sleep each night. I'd wake in the morning with her oracle cards spread across the breakfast table. She sang little German folk songs to me, which danced in my mind for the day. From rise to rest, there were no limitations to the wonder of this world and the next.

Even though she's now passed, my maternal grandmother and I hold a bond to last a lifetime. Her Aquarius rebellion was such an intrigue to me as a little girl. She came to visit us often. She'd let me stay up past my bedtime, even sneaking into my room to give me sips from her glass Coca-Cola bottle, which my mother denied me because sugar was apparently the devil. Oh, but my Oma Ernie didn't care. "*Such foolishness,*" she'd say in German and tell me to hurry as I sipped the sweet nectar, glancing over her shoulder to make sure my mother wasn't coming. I'd giggle and squeal with delight (or perhaps from the sugar overload), the happiest lil' Sagittarius in the world to be breaking the rules with my grandmother, then she'd shush me and tuck me back in.

As a teenager, I would fly across oceans to visit her. She'd sneak cigarettes in an old garden shed, sitting among the shovels and rakes on a comfortable wooden bench. I watched as the smoke slipped through the old wooden slats one day while eating blackberries in the old, whimsical garden of her German home, then opened the door. She jumped, yelled at me to come in and close the door behind me so no one would catch us, and offered me a puff. She thought she was so clever, hiding in that old tool shed in the garden—as if my grandfather didn't know what she was doing. She loved me so much. And I her.

Our world was rich with the delight of making up our own rules and breaking the ones anyone dared put on us. Oma Ernie's Aquarius nature didn't give a damn and took me by the hand to show me the way. I ran to keep up with her, hungry for the laughter she instilled and the mischief she allowed—all in the name of pure love.

She didn't speak English, except for the curse words I taught her—which she said with abandon. My little Sagittarius self was over the moon with delight. She filled my heart to the brim. There we were, cursing like sailors, sipping on Coca-Cola, smoking in the old tool shed, and laughing at the world.

On October 2, 2020, Oma Ernie joined the stars. I could feel her relief, as she had been disgruntled about still being alive well into her 90s. She was ready to go. I felt I became closer to her in her death, as there wasn't an ocean separating us anymore. She's laughing and smoking up on her cloud, telling the dirtiest jokes, cracking all the Angels up with her humor.

I carry the spirit of the women who have come before me in my lineage. I have a strong connection with my great-great-grandmother, Anna. I've never met her, but she lives in me. She's held me through my darkest days. I didn't realize it was her until I spoke to my mom about her presence—then, it all made sense. She's been a great protector of my boys and me.

FALLING IN LOVE WITH THE STARS

Somewhere along the way, I was given a golden key to a grand cosmic doorway, and I accepted. I put the key into the keyhole, entered the vast galaxy of stars and planets, and connected them to Earth.

In grocery stores of old, they'd have little wrapped-up scrolls for each zodiac sign at the checkouts, and of course, they caught my eye as my mom bagged our groceries. I'd beg her, "Please, Mom, just this one? Just this time?" I'd open the tiny scroll and find the magic of the stars, all things Sagittarius, unfold onto my lap. Reading in the backseat of our old 1970s powder-blue station wagon, my love for astrology began.

I discovered how those immense cosmic bodies affect us here on Earth. As the Moon pulls the tides, the planets pull at our psyche, our emotional bodies, our spiritual awareness, and even our physical bodies.

I fell in love. I danced with Neptune and fought with Mars. I spoke with Mercury until we were drunk on words. I sat up straighter for Saturn and gasped at the Moon's sovereignty. I applied all that they taught me down here in Earth school. *As above, so below.*

I've studied astrology deeply and will continue to do so until my last breath. I'd been practicing for thirty years before taking those studies and building my career. I now get to give countless readings to the most wonderful clients around the world and teach astrology classes online.

The twelve archetypes have always been rich with life for me. I meet people and take notes. I study them. I let them take my hand as they guide me into their birth chart. I step into their shoes and shapeshift into their cosmic truth. Neptune on my Sun allows me to do this with ease.

As a highly sensitive person, I feel the unseen and immediately pick up on people's energy. Show me a birth chart, and I know one's soul. I feel their sweet humanness—and also their cosmic promises.

Upon meeting, don't tell me your name—tell me your sign, especially your Moon Sign. *Then*, I can know you and understand you fully.

HOW TO USE THIS BOOK

There are many ways to use this book.

Start by reading your Sun Sign—which you probably already know. Then, move to your Moon Sign, and finally, read your Rising Sign (also known as the Ascendant).

These are the three pillars of your chart. The three primary energies you came here to express, whether outwardly (Sun Sign) or internally (Moon Sign). To know these three archetypes that live so profoundly within you is to know yourself. Knowing your cosmic promise is finding compassion and understanding for the self.

Your Sun, Moon, and Rising Signs—this is what astrologers call your "Big Three." Let me break them down.

Sun Sign: The Sun spends about thirty days in a zodiac sign. This is the sign the Sun was in on the day you were born, which becomes your Sun Sign, also known as your zodiac sign. The Sun Sign is your personality, character, and ego. Much like the Sun, it's the warm light you radiate out into the world. It is a core part of how you operate.

Your Sun Sign will find expression in all the ways you show up to the rhythms of your life. It's a sacred part of you—the celestial part. It's the creation of your essence from where you begin. Let your Sun Sign out to play often. She's not meant to be hidden. Embrace her. Know her. Adore her.

Others will notice your Sun Sign once they get to know you and see the way you move through the world. I say it's the most common part of you. I dream of a world where, upon meeting and sharing our first name, we also share our Sun Sign. *Hi, I'm Malika, Sagittarius.* Imagine knowing those core parts of yourself and being part of an everyday introduction. Before we can get there, though, astrology has to become more of a common language. Only time will tell.

Moon Sign: The Moon spends just two and a half days in a zodiac sign. The Moon Sign represents your inner life, emotions, and intuition. Your Moon Sign is everything you are when you come home at the end of the day and close the front door behind you. It's your personal life, innermost world, and moods. The Moon Sign represents how you express your emotions and emotionally react. Only those close to you will see and know your Moon Sign. To know and understand your Moon Sign is to love yourself. It's the most tender part of us that wants to be held and nurtured. That's why our Moon Sign shows up strongly in our personal relationships. It's how we reach out through the heart space and connect with others.

Some people feel more connected to their Moon Sign than their Sun Sign because it's much more personal. While some find their Moon Sign is quiet and hidden deeply within themselves, others shout their Moon Sign loud and proud (like anyone with a fire moon). Some of us wear our Moon (heart) on our sleeve. If you care deeply for someone, know their Moon Sign. Nurture their Moon. Love their Moon. It is, truly, their heart.

Rising Sign: The Rising Sign, also known as the Ascendant, is the constellation on the eastern horizon at the moment of your birth. You must know your birth time and place to determine your Rising Sign. This is your soul's promise and what your soul is rising up toward. This is also the mask you wear to the world. You may come across as your Rising Sign to those who don't know you personally. It's the first imprint we get from you as an acquaintance before we get to know you. We greet the world with our Ascendant. It rises from us with grace and soul. We enter the party with our Ascendant. It's like a nametag for strangers.

As children, we are often very much in our Ascendant and operate from the soulful promise we made in embodying it. Our Rising Sign is a big, comfortable part of us, and we exude it without inhibitions. Then, as life has its way, we tend to veer away from our Rising Sign in adult life, and it takes much more work to remember that promise our soul made, often requiring conscious effort.

In our adult years, we tend to default more toward our Sun Sign, as our lives are busy with work and our responsibilities in their many forms. The Rising Sign is still within us, but there's a certain amount of conscious reverence we should make toward it, to let it shine again just like our Sun, as it once did when we were kids. That usually happens when we allow life to slow down again in our elder years. There's a wholeness we reach when we embody our Ascendant, and it can feel quite delicious.

As we enter our elder years, there it is—our old friend, our Rising Sign. It's like a welcome home. We wrap it around us again, like a favorite old, worn sweater. She fits perfectly around our soft shoulders. We can relax into our Ascendant once again as our soul has the chance to settle down and exhale into her familiarity. The busy rush of life has quieted, and we come back to ourselves.

Our Rising Sign shows up in our physical bodies as well. It's our manner of movement, how we take up physical space on Earth, and our style. The Rising Sign is a whole damn vibe. It's the bridge from your Sun to your Moon. "See me!" shouts the Ascendant. And we do. It radiates from you. It's your soul coming out to play.

Think of your Big Three like this: You see a stranger in the grocery store choosing apples. The first hit you get from them is their Rising Sign—the mask they wear outside their home. Then, say you walk up to them, and they introduce themselves. Upon shaking their hand, you can see and feel their Sun Sign—their personality and character become present. Last, when they invite you over for a cup of tea, you can see and feel their Moon Sign—which they reveal only in their private realms.

Read the signs of your loved ones. This book will help you understand them and the archetype they came to express.

As the Sun shifts from sign to sign, you can also read what sign the Sun is visiting in real time. This will help you understand the energy and the lessons of that tale we all feel as a collective. Embody it, embrace it, and let it come to life within you as you dance with the giant cosmic clock in the sky.

Because the Moon transits through the zodiac so quickly, you may also want to discover the sign the Moon is moving through that day, read its tale, and use this as a meditative, reflective, and introspective practice. Ground yourself into that tale's story, and let it satiate your inner world. You can also practice this as we have New and Full Moons each month. Read the tale for the collective New Moon's and Full Moon's Signs and glean this cycle's wisdom.

In addition, if you're more advanced in astrology, you may also use this book according to your Progressed Moon, which is a two-and-a-half-year cycle. Knowing your Progressed Moon cycle helps you understand the very flavor of life you're living in for those two and a half years. Find the tale of the Progressed Moon Sign you're in and understand the essence of your life for this duration. Try to embrace that tale and embody its archetype. It's an invitation. It won't be around forever. Wring the juice from it while it's there.

Thank you for picking up this book. I hope you feel the core magic of your essence as you read your tale.

Tales of the Zodiac

AN ARIES TALE

The heat of you, as we approach, feels palpable.
    You are on fire.
    Unabashedly, you throw flames from the irises of your eyes.
My God, even the brave turn to ash under your gaze.

The sunset has nothing on you.

Your beauty rises from the seductive depths of hell, where you brought the devil, shaking, to his knees.

You step onto the battlefield, ready to fight for those you love.

The blood you collect on your sword tells the story of those who have wronged you. Those stupid enough to aim their weapons at you simply crumble as they meet your red-hot gaze.

With the back of your bloodied hand, you wipe the sweet nectar of victory from your lips as many times as you need to.

The ground shakes under your gait, leaving a scorch of heat on Earth as even she bows to your powerful presence.

Your mouth is the entrance to paradise. You taste like cinnamon and spice and everything not-so-nice. We beg you to seduce us, and just like the Fire Goddess you are, you seduce us straight into submission.

As you swing your hips and head our way, thunder rumbles, and we brace ourselves. Even the gods know you mean business.

You blaze into our lives fiercely, and once you've had your way with us, you sway your hips on the way out as you leave behind a trail of smoke, looking for the next thing to conquer.

You leave us breathless, and we must remind ourselves—we asked for this. If we look closely, we see our scars as evidence of your heat.

But it's a heat we can't resist, and we'll burn a million times over just to get another taste of you.

You're an inferno—a goddamn bonfire that we would only be so lucky to warm our cold hands on.

You are not for the faint of heart.

You show us the medicine of anger, of rage—the kind that burns in the very center of a flame. You show us how it propels you forward, and with the heat of your fire, potent transmutation takes place—the kind that only a starving soul would dare ask for.

You step into leadership roles when the rest of us need someone to look to. You take us by the hand and lead us to success, as you are our biggest cheerleader. You see the potential in everyone you love and won't let us settle for anything less.

When we become tired and worn down by life, you show up as the strength that gets us up off the couch and moving. You take our hand in yours, and suddenly, we are infused with courage, stamina, and drive. You're the one who propels us forward with your unwavering support.

You remind us of the power that resides within us and light our fire. You are the push we desperately need.

You teeter right on the edge of acceptable and dare us to push you over to the other side. With fire in your belly, you throw a lit match—burning bridges and laughing as we try to find a way to you, desperate for just a morsel of your powerful attention.

You scream at the stars when you don't get your way, and like us, they, too, bow down to your demands. You take your place at the throne—a warrior queen that takes up space unapologetically.

You demand to participate in this life. The scars you proudly wear are proof that you do just that. The bloodier the battle, the harder you fight. The more we attempt to silence you, the louder you get until your voice is all we can hear, ricocheting off the walls into a deafening roar.

We need time to recover from you. We toss and turn at night, remembering the impact of your passion. You've left your mark on us, and your memory is forever burned behind our closed eyelids. And that's exactly how you want it.

A TAURUS TALE

The sky turns moody as we catch the intoxicating scent of wildflowers. We know you are near.

You don't wear perfume to entice us—you exude the aroma of Mother Nature's sweet elixir as you walk by, and all sensibility falls away. Those of us who have had a taste of you can't get you off our tongue—for better or for worse.

We look into your eyes, and we are at your mercy. Your eyes hold the promise of spring as the soil beneath your feet keeps you steady and grounded. You dig your toes deeper, pulling Earth's anchor up through your being.

You look to the skies, wondering what it would be like to shake loose this anchor and float in the breeze. But you could never. Earth is your God. She holds your heart and devotion—and we all know, once devoted, a Taurus doesn't sway.

You measure your steps and calculate your plans. You create your world of beauty and tangible truths. You dream in the shadows and bring them to light. You find the seed beneath the garden's soil and coax it toward the Sun. You are the song the roots listen to—they reach, reach, reach toward your voice.

Even they can't help but grow from your love. And so you live your life, an enigma of softness and strength—a vision of calm with a storm inside.

You awaken our senses with the curve of your smile. You appear in our lives with a sultry presence as untamed as your soul. Your wild hair whips around as even the wind can't keep her hands off you.

The sky cracks open, and we can't help but look up at you with awe. You have come from the center of Mother Earth, holding all her secrets and wisdom in your hands.

Your hands—soil beneath your fingernails only makes you look more glamorous. You caress the flowers and trees just as you caress our hearts. Your hands carry wood, carry stones, carry rivers—your hands hold the medicinal wisdom that saves our very lives.

You build us shelter. The heat of the Sun doesn't stop you. You collect Earth's resources and work with them as though they're an intrinsic part of you. Your hands work the mud as the Sun, your assistant, bakes it into clay. The trees lend you their branches for wood. You collect the tall grasses that bend to your beauty to use as straw after the heat has its way with them. Long after we've grown weary and tired, you build on. You've never shied away from hard work, and it shows.

We want to roll in your satin sheets with you in the heat of summer, even though we know we can't keep you past autumn.

You belong to no man. You belong to Earth herself. You belong to the wind, the waters, the soil, the roots of existence. You are the Medicine Mama, coming to heal our human wounds with your salves and magic spells, carried on your breath in a whisper, right into our ears. We heal in your wake.

You make love to us, you feed and nurture us, and you leave us shaking and begging for more of you.

Your voice hypnotizes. Your elegant throat elicits the hymn of Angels singing in a choir. You awaken our sense of sound, and nothing compares to your voice . . . your voice . . . your voice. It haunts us long after you've left us and returned to nature, your first true love.

You invite us to dine at your table, and we become drunk with your offerings. There will always be dessert held out to us, from your tongue into our eager mouths. We can still taste the sweet nectar of dining with you, even when it becomes just a memory.

You dance in the breeze like a whimsical flower, but we all know you're anything but whimsical. You're a force to be reckoned with.

You appreciate the finer things in life, but you've worked yourself to the bone—bloodied and worn—to get them.

Self-indulgence is a tattoo you wear on your suntanned skin because we all know there's such a thing as overindulging in the richness of life—and you're here for it.

"More . . ." you whisper to the sky, and she delivers. "More . . . MORE . . ." you demand of Venus, and she supplies. You are intoxicated with the finer things of life, unashamed, and invite us to plunge into your bathtub of pearls.

You've built this life. You deserve the Venusian blessings you collect and swim in. You always knew, in the end, no one was coming to save you, so you saved your own damn self.

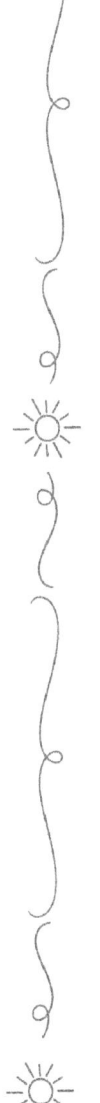

A Gemini Tale

You don't go the speed limit. You rev your engine and travel a thousand miles an hour, daring us to keep up with you.

You are a lighthouse in the distance as we seek refuge in your presence. Your light shines through the darkest night, guiding us.

Constant movement. You won't hold still for long—no, that's not how you flow. You flit from flower to flower, gathering your information to build your empire of stars.

You weave together words and wisdom and deliver them to your castle of people, who eagerly await your return, hoping your light might shine on them next.

You are a child at the adult's table and wouldn't want it any other way. Peter Pan at heart, you'll never be compared to a stuffy adult—*where's the fun in that?* You make a promise to never grow up.

You tickle us with your lightness of being and use our laughter as sails to bring you to your next curious adventure.

Mischievous eyes are part of your outfit. When you turn them on us, we get giddy with excitement, begging you to grab us by the hand and take us with you.

And we're off to the outermost galaxies, hand in hand, where you show us things we've never dreamed of.

You wither in the face of stagnation. You would lie down and beg to die at the foot of boredom. So, you keep moving—too fast for us.

Somehow, you make a hot mess look good. You damn near make it look sexy. Your hands never stop moving, and we can only dream that you'll play us like a piano.

The wind—your first lover—makes garments flutter like linen against your willowy body. You are a breath of fresh air, and we get drunk off your breeze.

"Look!" you say. "Keep your eyes open . . ." And we do—because we trust you. And with you by our side, we behold the wonders of the world. You won't bother with anything short of amazing.

You take your finger, briefly touch our third eye, and we are awakened. You don't want us to miss a beat.

The use of words is the only sword you'll need. You blast them at us and hit your target before we even think to duck. You don't miss—no, you don't ever miss.

Your wild tongue licks the skin off our bones when you feel wronged. You lash us with wit and wisdom. Your mind is crystalline precision. We will never be a match for your intelligence.

The fountain of youth provides your beverages, which you delicately sip from as others surrounding you look on. Your ethereal beauty is a sight to behold.

Just when we think we know you, you delightfully surprise us. Those of us who want to keep hold of you have another thing coming. You slip through our fingers—gracefully, elegantly—and before we know it, you're gone.

You won't be held down. You don't stay for long. There are too many who need you, who inspire you, who want to breathe you in.

We were the lucky ones to have been met by your presence.

Your laughter still echoes within our four walls. Your lipstick stain remains on the coffee mug. So we sit, wait, and pray we'll see you again in some galaxy, on some star, as you roam the world in search of understanding.

Will you return? Only time will tell.

A CANCER TALE

As you kiss the spring winds goodbye, you bring the heat of the summer sun and take your place on the silver throne. You arrive from the past as you step elegantly into our lives. You feel like the ocean—a healing presence that gives life and can just as easily destroy.

Unrequited love is part of your story, and you keep the mementos under your bed—a box of past lovers you drove mad with your nectar skin and moon eyes. Your aching soul relishes in the lovers you've collected.

A honey-scented, nostalgic air moves about your frame as you walk with an army of ancestors by your side. Your great-grandmother's locket takes its place around your neck, igniting your feminine power. Her presence is palpable around you.

This lineage you come from has brought you to your knees time and time again as you pull your strength from them and bring forth healing. You pray at the altar of your grandmothers, bowing deeply to the women who have come before you. You battle family traumas that were never yours to fight in the first place. All in the name of holy, sacred ancestral healing.

You hold your daughter's hands, and her daughters' and their daughters', whispering the thirteen wisdoms into their ears as you birth within them the wisdom of the witch.

The waves have thrust you about until you felt battered and broken, only to be held in the arms of your feminine lineage—cradled until you felt whole again. You are the most resilient of us—shaped and changed by the waves as they lap around you, over you, within you.

You part our parched lips and pour the waters of your soul into us. You make us your family. As we enter your inner circle, we will forever be protected by you. Damned are those who threaten your loved ones. They've never seen the wrath of you. It's an unforgettable sight, and if they're able to get up and walk away, your lessons will forever shape the rest of their lives.

You are vintage—a buried chest of treasure we have been lucky enough to find. With eager eyes and hands, we dig into you, hopeful of the wealth we'll find in being loved by you.

You are the ocean's apprentice. You move your body like the waves that lap at our toes and draw us in, deeper, deeper.

You are the quintessential Mother—the matriarch of the family. You keep the stories of your lineage alive. You keep the secrets of the family tucked away until they make you sick—until they choke you.

Then, in the name of healing, they come out. You turn to the Moon and whisper them into the night until the whispers turn to a howl, exploding from your ribcage, turning you inside out with vulnerability.

The tears that come only make you stronger. You show us what it means to be so fucking alive with emotion that we shiver in the witnessing.

The Moon is on your payroll. She works for *you*. It was you—you are the one who taught the Moon how to control the tides, how to pull from them, how to release them back into the great Mother.

You don't dance on the surface but beg to be overtaken until you reach the very bottom—pulling from the depths, clawing at the sand as you reach the river's floor. You come up for air, bruised from the river's lashing, and laugh with the pain of it. You see, while we fear pain and raw emotion—you thrive in it.

You find God there.

You take that pain, sorrow, and yearning and build your moon-silver castle. You call us to you—the people you love. We gather close. It's lavender honey on our tongue, the taste of you.

You take your place on the silver throne. All is illuminated by moonlight as we eagerly sip from the sea's saltwater you offer us in a ruby cup, forever binding us to you. With a glint in your eye, you watch us gulp greedily, not knowing it will have us coming back for more.

We are at your mercy, hypnotized by you—the ultimate feminine goddess.

Even if we wanted to pull away, we can't.

Because once you love us, you will never let us go.

A LEO TALE

Y ou take your position on the throne as if you were born for it—and you were. We can't help but bow down at your feet.

The Sun fuels your power. Some of us look up to you—others are jealous of all you are. The jealousy projected on you only makes you more powerful. "Bring it on," you say, with a low growl in your belly. "I dare you."

You spend your days fostering your inner child with the love you crave. The weight of your crown cramps your neck, and you get bored of our worship. You rip it from your head, and you beg us to play with you like a child. Because that is your true nature—God-like and child-like—they're the same for you.

Your creative process is like no other—paint streaked across your arms, glitter in your hair, fire in your eyes.

Like the Sun, you don't give a damn if you blind us. Many have to look away—the light you carry within you is like God turning on a million suns at once.

Your mouth is the entrance to our own personal Garden of Eden. Your heart is made of an ancient golden fire.

You won't settle for the bare minimum. You want the Sun and the Moon. You want the ache of a broken heart repaired by another's hands who lives for you and you alone. You want to romance the fuck out of your life. You'll have it no other way.

You dream of a love so saturating it makes your teeth throb—you're starving for it. And we ask you . . . do you really want love? Or just the soothing medicine of knowing you're lovable?

The world is at your calling. Even she can't slow you down, hold you back, or stop your fire from blazing. This is what you've been preparing for—propelling yourself into the greatness of all that you are—which is absolutely everything all at once.

We observe in awe. We hear you roar like a lioness when you feel wronged. We listen to you purr like a kitten when you are pleased—and we crave to hear that purr from our doing.

So, we lean into the madness of loving you. Your eyes on us send shivers up and down our spine. We eat from your hand, begging for more. Being loved by you is like winning the lottery of life. Your love holds us by the throat as we follow in your wake, begging you to turn around and see us.

To be you is to perform. You want to be a celebrity, yet unknown. You crave the spotlight yet purr in the dark. You want to be center stage, yet hidden among the wildflowers, blending in until we don't know the difference between you and a majestic sunflower.

You shield your eyes as the curtains lift and the lights shift to you, as you stand solo on stage, being the main character of this life. This is a big ask. Who else but you can step into it? A fear of the dark, you will never shy away from the lights. A fear of being nameless, you will make sure everyone remembers who you are—king of the world.

You are the untamed child. The wonder of this life never ceases to amaze you as you touch what you've been told not to and enter where you were forbidden to go. This is you. You will not be told what to do. You came in with a lion's heart, fearless and stubborn, brave and wild.

Your past lovers live between your teeth, in the rise of your hips, underneath your fingernails—and we know we'll be making our bed there, eventually.

We take what we can from you while we can—while we have you. We take a piece of you that was never ours to begin with.

And so you walk the world, replenishing your fire, gathering more kindling for your heart, and containing the pieces of your spark so they don't cause a wildfire.

We beg you not to subdue the spark. You're exhausted from the work.

Raise your arms and let your fire rage and roar around us. We want to be dancing in your flame, turned orange from the light it casts into the shadows, until we ourselves become transmuted by the alchemy of you.

A VIRGO TALE

You descend from the stairway of heaven, coming down to be with us here on Earth. You are—in our eyes—our Earth Angel.

You are Divinity. You love our darkness back into light. Effortlessly.

You're quick. We can't keep your pace. You zip from galaxy to galaxy, dust off the stars, straighten the asteroids, and keep Mercury neat and tidy.

You march into our messy lives and see what's not working. And you go about setting things right—selflessly, with a passion in which we feel fully loved.

You don't want to see how handsome or how fancy our clothes are—you only want to see our bookshelves—catching glimpses of our inner story, our inner world, what fascinates us, and where our mind dwells.

You've trained us to speak our own name with kindness, gentleness, and compassion. You've taught us the purity of love that oozes from your very fingertips. You've guided us on how to return to the purest form of our being.

You've not always been this way. You had to swim through the mud until you felt like your lungs were filling with lotus flowers—while pretty, you couldn't breathe. You had to bite your tongue in the face of ego, of suffering, of cruelty.

They told you that you had to be perfect. You had to get it right. It was all a lie.

You throw your coffee cups against the wall with a satisfying shatter. You rip your clothes off their hangers and toss them about until your hair slips out of its top knot . . . until you look like a wild thing. You leave your bed unmade. Just to see the world didn't end. They lied. And you laugh. *Free at last.*

It took many Moons to undo the stories you've been told about yourself, all the lies they shed, to be able to walk barefoot upon this Earth and claim your right to be here. Because you do belong. Every tree bows down to you, their roots begging for your feet to walk across them. Every flower turns her face toward your light, your beauty, and she stands a little taller.

It took you years to find the courage to claim your space among the stained humans who make such messes and silly mistakes.

You came back to the desk to rewrite your story. You washed off the mud, pulled the lotus out of your lungs by the roots—and breath returned.

You put things in order—found chaos and created a system of ease and flow. It's not been easy. But you pushed through the hard work because nobody was showing up to save you. You saved yourself.

To be loved by you is to be showered with the most graceful, loyal, steadfast love. We can finally lean into a solid form—you, always unwavering. No detail of our heart goes unnoticed by you. You spoil us, and we take advantage. We are not worthy of this love.

You make love like you are separating the stars from space—the sand from the ocean. You fulfill us, until the insatiable become satiated. It is nothing short of the sacred unearthing of our souls, to be in union with you.

You are a quote we will never forget.

We look up to you, thinking, "*God has sent the One.*" And you become the One. The love of our life. The One who got away. The One who holds our trembling hearts in your able hands, bringing healing, bringing peace, bringing salvation.

You sigh . . . tired. Exhausted from this mess. Why must you always be the one to set things right? There are times when you feel unseen in all your efforts, resentful, and threaten to throw in the towel if we don't start appreciating you. It doesn't last long. You retie the laces on your boots and get started on your next task. You can't help it.

These tasks are of the heart. You couldn't stop helping even if you tried your damnedest.

At the end of your day, you curl into the cloud God has fluffed for you, singing lullabies of old into your ear as She straightens your halo.

You are, after all, her favorite child.

A LIBRA TALE

Electricity crackles in the air. We watch, breathless, as you float down our street. Are your feet even touching the earth? You move so gracefully, as if the air propels you forward, no anchor, straight into our hearts. We can feel the static cling of our garments and hair as you approach. We stop what we do as you make a grand entrance.

Oh, Venus had her way with you. That we can clearly see—a face that has been sculpted with the finest clay Venus could find. She chose her finest pen and drew her masterpiece the day she made you. Under your beauty, there's a nervous edge, a gnawing of the bones that won't leave you alone for long. You're worried that we won't love you when the beauty fades. You needn't worry—it's a beauty as timeless as time itself. It has no end and no beginning.

To lay eyes upon you is like watching the Venusian glow of the sunset, in the pure ecstasy of the moment, begging summer to stay as we lick the sticky, sweet juice of nectarines off our fingers. You are breathtaking, and we can't pull our gaze away. We want to consume you and claim you for our own. You come from autumn itself. You wring the last drops of summer from the Sun as the winds pick up. An endless October sets in, where we dream of a love like yours to feed us through the cold winter months ahead. We pray for time to stop.

The symphony of your love song fills our ears, and we greedily turn up the volume until you're all we hear. You, your song, moving through our blood until we can't figure out where we end and you begin—and that's how you want it. But you are restless. There's that music again, playing just for you, and you must move your body to its beat.

They told you to be a good girl. They strung ribbons in your curled hair. Put you in the prettiest dress. Told you to be seen and not heard. They told you to put everyone before you. They trimmed your wings. They trimmed and trimmed until, one day, they clipped them completely.

You listened. Eager to please. You used your manners. You said what they wanted to hear. You created no waves. You kept that boat steady, so steady, until you were scared your own breath might rock it. The titles and expectations they piled upon you make most forget that you came here to be a force.

Your true voice lay forgotten, tossed in the corner, along with the bouquets from old lovers in spiderwebs of dust. You blended in with all the other pleasantries you spouted when prompted until you lost yourself. Until the very air you were birthed from became still. You lay on the ground, unmoving. How could you move when they took the melody away? Silenced your music?

You've longed for the love of your life to come in and save you. Never realizing, until now, that you are the love of your life. You are who you've been waiting for all along. Then, as the summer comes to an end, you start to move out of sheer, cardinal will—to claim back everything you lost when you merged into who they told you to be.

The air swirls. As does your anger. You summon the winds from the four directions. You call them in. They swirl around you, stronger and stronger, until you've created a tornado that destroys your silence and agreeable words. It destroys the pretty dresses and tatters your hair ribbons to shreds. But it doesn't kill you.

This windstorm gives you your life back. You become the eye of your own storm. You embody your cardinal air until you can't ever be tamed again. Your wind whips around us, daring us to stifle and quiet you into agreeable nods. Our eyes water, our hair flies wild. You are a force to be reckoned with.

When you find your voice, it booms like thunder. We didn't know. We had no idea of the strength one soul could hold. You scream profanities and laugh at our shocked faces as "no" becomes your favorite word. You start putting yourself first. Imagine that. Honey drips from your hips as you meet us, renewed, recharged, and never again lying beneath anyone. Once again, you become sweet as pie, and we become addicted to your sugar. Under your spell, we forget—even the prettiest flowers have thorns.

You'll never have a chest that doesn't hold the ache of love lost—a lover's residue, faded into the dusky sky at sunset. You want to tell us your love story without naming yourself as a character. You separate to spare yourself the pain. You share the story of love that lives in your head. Perhaps one day, it'll live in your heart, too.

You want to know what it's like to be served so much love on your dinner plate that you don't have to plead for seconds. We beg for the privilege of lying beside you, holding your head of dreams and stories in our lap—to dream under the same Moon. You leave end-of-summer blackberry stains on our mouths as you smile sweetly and kiss our hungry lips. We know you'll love us and leave us, but we can't help but beg to be the one to keep you warm for just one more night.

A SCORPIO TALE

You emerge from the darkness of the lake, shaking the water from your hair. The serpent wraps herself around your upper arm like an amulet—this is your chosen jewelry.

Our hands shake as we approach you, our teacher, to guide us into the dance with the shadow. It's a sultry dance, as you've mastered the art of seduction. You never break eye contact as your hips sway side to side while we strive to look anywhere but within your powerful eyes. We know the risk. We know what the hypnosis your eyes alone can bring.

If we look, we're afraid we'll fall madly, deeply in love with you. You smile, amused, and slowly raise your cup to your lips, drinking the sweet nectar of your latest victim, hoping that we'll be next.

You lead us into the underworld, the illuminating shadows guiding your way. As the monsters gnash their teeth, you turn to sit with them. You slip your hand in theirs, acknowledge them, and they shrink before you. Suddenly, you are their God. You move into the darkest corners of Earth, bringing your inner light.

Burrowed light isn't your thing. You take up the match. You strike it. And you stoke the fire within yourself. The darker the room, the brighter your fire blazes. You cast aside shadows after you've had your taste of them, their echo still churning in your gut. When your obsessions reach a boiling point, you drink them in, the heat of the water sizzling off your tongue, unscathed.

You kiss us with this tongue—you taste of heartache and battle, of worlds forgotten, of magic and depth. You claim us with this tongue. We lose resistance, and we are yours. We try to dilute you, to make you easier to swallow. You throw your head back and laugh at this idea. You stand strong in your convictions and intensity. Full flavor. The ultimate spice. Those who can't handle it weren't meant for you anyway.

You made a promise to know Death intimately. You've sat at many a bedside, holding Death's hand, watching transition and transformation. With you by our side, we know we can do hard things.

"Save us . . . Save us . . ." we beg of you when the intensity gets too loud, when the water rises over our head and we feel like we're drowning. But no, you don't save us. You wouldn't dream of it. You show us more and that we're stronger than the wound. You show us how to demand our power back unto ourselves, and with that, we survive another day.

Your throat is raw from screaming into the abyss, and when the abyss screams back, you saturate your skin with it. You scream for us, for humanity, for life after death. The body you occupy is the body of a survivor. The stories you've moved through aren't for the weak. You came in with a big promise—in the face of death, to become even more alive—in the face of darkness, to become the brightest of lights.

You are Pluto's child and his proudest creation. You teach us how to reach a boiling point. You are water, but you're not the stillness of a lake at dusk. You are a lake set on fire. The water boils. The heat transmutes. You, yourself, are often mistaken for fire. But if we look beyond our burned fingertips from touching you, we see the waves lapping at the shore of stillness and calm. You pull us in with your riches. You whisper spells forgotten. You wield power envied, and you remind us who the fuck we are.

Blood doesn't run through your veins—desire does. Longing does. And so you go after what you crave, what you obsess about, until you have possession of it. You do so quietly, stealthily. You don't need an audience. You feast on your desire won until your soul's teeth feel satiated from the chewing.

We build dreams about you. We fantasize about you. We love you into our ruin. But you see, that's what you want from us. You wouldn't have it any other way. The deeper, the more soulful, the more you come alive. You are here to burn it all to the ground and make something brilliant from the ashes. And you do. So brilliant, we can hardly stand it. We don't remember the alchemy, but we know there was blood.

And so you go on, the clever creature who turns herself into the very epitome of healing. You sit with us in our darkness, and your presence is quiet yet powerful. You can sit with us because you have gone through the same storm, once upon a dark night of the soul, and you wouldn't dream of us traveling alone.

And so, because of you, we can go on. You pull us from the destruction and show us how to fly. You show us your scars and the lessons you learned from them. You show us how to breathe underwater. And with that breath, we resurrect. When another battle comes your way, you sigh, bored—this existence is exhausting. You've died a hundred deaths in one lifetime, so what's another?

A SAGITTARIUS TALE

You preach from the pulpit as you curse into the wind. You wink at the nuns as you walk past, daring them to say something as you saunter out the church doors, stubbing your cigarette out with the toe of your boot.

Ready or not, here you come. With feathers in your hair, you drop bombs of truth on us. You aim your arrow, never missing your shot. You hit your target every time. Whether that arrow is plunged into the poison of the hydra's blood or dipped in Cupid's elixir, we'll never know until it hits us—until it's too late.

Sometimes, love is not enough. You want more. You want to taste the grit of life. You want to rub it into your skin until it makes you raw, until you feel something. You show up in a ripped sundress, ready to erupt into flames. The heat licks at your heels as you burn toward us.

You purposely slip something of yours under each bed you bless. You dare your lovers to forget you. They'll remember you on those lonely nights, but you are far gone—off toward the horizons where the Sun is setting—and all they can see is your silhouette, shaped into the flames of chaos.

Heaven is a place on Earth when we're around you. We feel forever young when you sprinkle your laughter around us. It lands on our heads and gathers around our feet like the last leaves falling off the trees as your winter approaches.

We find you in the classrooms of life, teaching us from your bag of tricks that you've gathered from this big, wide world. We find you in the back alleys, sharing drinks with the mavericks and tricksters. You collect their life experience in your bag and use it when needed. You are the holy one. You are the renegade. You are the sting of spice that sets our tongues on fire.

You've loved sailors and saints. You've graced the tables of queens and peasants. You've slept with prophets and vagabonds. And you collect and collect and collect—forever seeking, forever wandering. You smell of burned incense and crushed roses.

You dream so big. We smirk and say, "Never. Impossible. Outrageous." Our declaration simply fuels your fire, and off you go, proving us wrong once again. You come back after many moons, dragging behind the carcass of your dreams, to show us that you've embodied the very life and drunk the blood from that dream.

You've wrung every last drop of juice from it. You've sucked the marrow out of its bones until you've had your fill, until you feel satisfied, until you've accomplished what we never thought you could.

We dance the night away with you, drunk on your inspiration and obsessed with your skin that glows in the moonlight. Have you cursed us or blessed us? You keep us guessing as you nip your teeth at our earlobe and grin into our eyes. You make us giggle in the most inappropriate places. You speak when you shouldn't. You point when it's impolite. And yet we crave you. We crave to get into delicious trouble with you because we know it'll be the highlight of our rebellion.

When the world gets too heavy, too serious, you throw your head back and laugh. You grab our hand and leap onto the carousel, and we spin around and around in your laughter, the fun-house music on repeat until we're sick to our stomachs and dizzy with your exuberance.

You lick the cotton-candy sugar off your fingertips, looking for the next ride to board. Your love gets stuck in our throats, and no amount of water can clear it. You rip free from restrictions. You are nobody's daughter. Certainly not your mother's.

You seek refuge in your God, as you always do, dancing wildly in her arms as She whispers the world's wisdom right into your ear. You beg forgiveness at her feet—the only feet you will ever bow down to.

You left through the garden gate one Thursday when you were endlessly restless. The caged bird beat against your ribs so hard you had to set her free. We're pressed against the window, searching through the December fog for your reappearance on the horizon. The pines echo your laughter, reminding us of your love's absence.

You are always on the run, yet with an enormous need to find your home. So you make your home in others' hearts, in others' beds, in others' bones. You plead for us to need you and live without you. This is what we stay alive for—to hear your stories upon your return, to feel your hungry lips meet ours as we taste everyone you've kissed along the way before you returned to us. You carry their stories on those lips, ready to spill them onto the plates we're ravenous to eat from.

We don't know who we'll get upon your return—the wild, impulsive, chaotic one? Or the contemplative, philosophical, quiet one? Will we even find out before you leave again? Probably not, and that's the price we're willing to pay to be loved by you.

A CAPRICORN TALE

You are a tale as old as time. An ancient soul, your newborn skin serving as a cover. We happily give our richest treasures and stand in the longest line to receive the wisdom that spouts from your lips. Over time, this wisdom has become embedded in your skin.

Life hasn't always been easy for you. Long ago, you had to leave your adolescence behind to show up as an adult. You stepped into the role of the parent, the guide, and the teacher for those who should have been holding *you*, guiding *you*.

You did this without complaint, as if you were born for this work. The adult in a little body. You pull from the strength that's always buzzing at your core, which has come from many lifetimes gathered—many ancient civilizations experienced.

Alone in a dark room, you've wept for your suffering, thirsty for the moisture the tears brought. But not for long. You knew you were stronger than the sorrow, and you got up and got up again to move toward your growth.

There is no other way. You bring the delicious darkness of winter with you, blowing in like the first snowstorm, as we turn inward with you. You show us how to light the candle. You guide us to find the light within. You keep us warm through the shorter days and darker months. So inside we go, with you guiding the way.

With you by our side, we find the tenacity to take care of our livelihood. You show us what it means to show up—for ourselves, for our promises, for the hard work you never shy away from.

Saturn's child, you make hard work look easy. You make it look like you're doing a dance with God. Simple steps, natural movements, with such grace that always lead you to the top.

When you arrive at success, you stand tall with pride. You knew you'd get there. *We* knew you'd get there. You reach your hand down to meet ours, reaching up toward you. Because you recognize it's lonely at the top, and human connection is, really, a desire that you strive for.

You gather us around you, as the mountain holds you, as the trees bend toward you, as Earth sighs with pleasure at your touch. You command nature, just as you command our attention.

We receive the words you teach, the wisdom you share, with hungry eyes. We gasp with pleasure as you stain our bodies with your knowing.

You've chosen your beloved. Graced are they who get to share your bed. Your body is a map of pleasure itself that you don't share with just anyone. Oh no, we have to pass tests and show the worthiness of your time and love.

There is a lasting love in the way you love us. We feel safe, knowing we can lean in on you, and the last thing you would do is topple over. This love comes from the center of Earth herself—sure, strong, stable. You become our language. You become our winter sky. You become our exhale. You bring us back to life in the coldest season.

You belong to no one, only Mother Time. She rolls down your back as you age gracefully, an elder in true form. You age backward—the first part of life has asked so much of you. Your spine throbs with remembrance. The heavy lifting. The hunger to figure it out, to get it right. Working to keep the family together, to keep your life together. You did it all.

But oh, how sweet the shift into middle age. You move a little freer. You laugh a little louder. And you allow the indulgences to have their way—just a little more. You let the lust of life leave its mark on your skin. Who knew life could be so delicious if we just moved with the rhythms?

As you approach the title of the Crone, you start wearing your crown unapologetically. We gaze at you in awe, love pouring out of our mouths, washing over you. We wonder if there was ever a time you didn't wear your crown. Weren't you born with it all along?

The softness sets in. There you are. Your touch softens and gentles. It heals the deepest wounds in us—those hands. Those hands that hold ancient Earth energy, when laid upon us, remedy us right back into wholeness.

We miss you as soon as we fall in love with you. Because we know, one day, another mountain will be calling your name. It'll be the highest mountain yet. And off you must go to answer its calling, just as you've answered the call of our hearts. Because after we are loved by you, we will never have a heart that won't ache.

AN AQUARIUS TALE

Our sweet, brilliant one—the air sizzles and cracks with electricity to announce your arrival. The hair stands up on the back of our necks—our necks that strain to see you, see the brilliance that is you.

You grab society's rule book and burn it to ashes in the fires of Vesta. You didn't listen to your parents, so why would you ever listen to rules others try to impose upon you? We gasp, shocked by your actions, and you beam with pride. The louder our gasp, the wider your smile.

We tried to teach you obedience, but the joke was on us. You are here to wake us up. You grab us by the shoulders and shake us until we see the light and the sense you're trying to inject into the world. Your electric soul wakes us up to the truth, to stark reality, and to your genius mind.

You show us nonconformity. You show us individuality. You grab our hand and lead us into the future, the new, progressive pathways we didn't see before you arrived. Born of a Uranian mind—we ask questions, and you provide the answers.

Long ago Saturn's child, before Uranus grabbed you for her own, you flip-flop between honoring tradition and blowing it all away by the touch of your tornado. Your moves are often misunderstood—you've been shunned and made to be the outcast. You've been called cold, detached, unemotional. But oh, how your heart aches with agony when people fail to see the real you.

Your heart bleeds for community and humanity in all forms. You give the dress off your back on the coldest of days. To hell with that dress anyway—you want to try on many gowns, like you do experiences, to see which one fits your oddity best, to find which one you can relax into for a bit.

You are fueled by air and adrenaline. We try to catch you, but Uranus has you moving at the speed of light, far beyond our reach.

Being human is one of your biggest challenges. You don't fit this skin. Your bones clunk around uncomfortably. Your soul searches for the exit door. You long for the world you came from before you came to Earth.

The anxiety that runs through your veins tries to push its way out of your body. It propels you forward, searching for your kind—searching for someplace to rest, to tenderly hold this heightened nervous system of yours. Is it the anxiety or boredom that makes your skin itch?

The queen of freedom, you'll change your address just so we can't catch you. You keep the mystery of you alive. You eat liberation for breakfast, lunch, and dinner. What goes too long untouched by wind, unmoved, becomes stagnant and destroys itself. You would rather die than exist at the feet of familiarity. Familiarity feels suffocating and old. So you throw open the windows and let the storm rage through the house, rearranging the furniture with its power.

AN AQUARIUS TALE

Our sweet, brilliant one—the air sizzles and cracks with electricity to announce your arrival. The hair stands up on the back of our necks—our necks that strain to see you, see the brilliance that is you.

You grab society's rule book and burn it to ashes in the fires of Vesta. You didn't listen to your parents, so why would you ever listen to rules others try to impose upon you? We gasp, shocked by your actions, and you beam with pride. The louder our gasp, the wider your smile.

We tried to teach you obedience, but the joke was on us. You are here to wake us up. You grab us by the shoulders and shake us until we see the light and the sense you're trying to inject into the world. Your electric soul wakes us up to the truth, to stark reality, and to your genius mind.

You show us nonconformity. You show us individuality. You grab our hand and lead us into the future, the new, progressive pathways we didn't see before you arrived. Born of a Uranian mind—we ask questions, and you provide the answers.

Long ago Saturn's child, before Uranus grabbed you for her own, you flip-flop between honoring tradition and blowing it all away by the touch of your tornado. Your moves are often misunderstood—you've been shunned and made to be the outcast. You've been called cold, detached, unemotional. But oh, how your heart aches with agony when people fail to see the real you.

Your heart bleeds for community and humanity in all forms. You give the dress off your back on the coldest of days. To hell with that dress anyway—you want to try on many gowns, like you do experiences, to see which one fits your oddity best, to find which one you can relax into for a bit.

You are fueled by air and adrenaline. We try to catch you, but Uranus has you moving at the speed of light, far beyond our reach.

Being human is one of your biggest challenges. You don't fit this skin. Your bones clunk around uncomfortably. Your soul searches for the exit door. You long for the world you came from before you came to Earth.

The anxiety that runs through your veins tries to push its way out of your body. It propels you forward, searching for your kind—searching for someplace to rest, to tenderly hold this heightened nervous system of yours. Is it the anxiety or boredom that makes your skin itch?

The queen of freedom, you'll change your address just so we can't catch you. You keep the mystery of you alive. You eat liberation for breakfast, lunch, and dinner. What goes too long untouched by wind, unmoved, becomes stagnant and destroys itself. You would rather die than exist at the feet of familiarity. Familiarity feels suffocating and old. So you throw open the windows and let the storm rage through the house, rearranging the furniture with its power.

Damned are those who fall in love with you and want to claim you as their own. You see, you could never love just one of us. Your heart is too big. You care for all. You have too much love to limit it to one soul's receival.

We think of little else but you. When you've left us out of sheer boredom, you still want everything to remind us of you. We cry to our next lover over you. Over and over. Until they know you as we knew you, until our lover, who's never met you, becomes your lover, too, by proxy.

You do not have to be wanted or agreed with to prove you exist. We feel your existence in the echo of you ringing through our ears—the memory of you bouncing against the barrier of our minds. You challenge us. You question our thoughts and our way of thinking. You defy our perceptions. You dare us to stand up for what we believe in. You scream NO from the top of your lungs—just for the pleasure of screaming.

January turns into February, and you have hope in your purpose. You tie back your wild hair, pull on boots over your mismatched socks, and go out to serve the masses. You feed the hungry, you protect the innocent, you scare away the bullies—all in the name of humanity. Your cry for justice as the fortress walls crumble.

You move through back alleys and darkened bar rooms, searching for the misfits, the outcasts, the outraged, and you gather your army. You carry the world on your back, along with all its people. Your activism will save us, as you fall to bloodied knees, if it's the last thing you do.

We second guess the revolution you bring. "What if it all goes wrong?" we cry, shaking from the task of joining your war. You pause, let your sword of justice swing down by your side, and look us right in the eye and challenge, "What if it all goes right?"

A PISCES TALE

We slip through the beads hanging in the doorframe as your hookah smoke curls into the air around you. The smoke clears. There you are. Hallelujah. A sight to behold.

Your ocean eyes shine directly onto us. If we come one step closer, we fear we might drown in them. To hell with fear, it's worth it—we step closer. We surrender to your waves as they crash against our ribs, and your siren song calls the loudest of all. We are in—treading water in the deepest part of your ocean. You are pure magic. You are the salt waters and the heavens combined.

You reach out your hand, and we submit. We go under the surface with you and are surprised to find that we can breathe here. The Angels whisper around you as you perform your fish magic.

Neptune's daughter, the one who promised to reach beyond the veils and dance with the heavens. The one who talks to her dead grandmother and still smells her perfume in the air.

You keep a jar of hearts on your bookshelf, right next to your poetry, of all the loves you've had. You admire the way the Sun kisses the window, the way the dust mites dance in the air, just as you dance in the marrow of our bones.

You wear skin that isn't yours, as Neptune has you merging and sighing into your next lover. You ask for a container to pour yourself into so that you may take shape, and we provide. Anything to keep you from slipping through our fingers.

We dream of you. You are our favorite hiding place. We don't remember falling in love with you. It felt like a dream that evaporated in the morning light. We just know that if we have to let go, it will hurt like hell. There will be scars, and there will be tears. The loneliness you leave us with after you're gone is more loyal than you. We wake, having forgotten your face. The dream of you has collected at our feet, and we wade through it as we go about our day. All we know is we are hungry for you.

You've searched for yourself for so long. You feel, you suffer, you cry. You became a storm cloud. How many people are you? Who are you? This never-ending space between you and you. You can't let go of the people you used to be, so you carry them all. They are all you, until you are nothing but chaos and space. You carry a sorrow in your soul that you can't shake free. Why must the world feel so heavy? Why does it all land within you?

You were told you were too sensitive. Too deep. Too rich with feeling. Too whimsical. Too quiet. Too passive. Too much. Too weak. Too strong. So what did you do with this? You froze your water. You froze your tears. You froze your heart for protection. Frozen so you could feel normal and survive this world. You simply . . . existed.

As your fingertips turned blue, you brought them toward the fire to warm them. The flame melted the frozen bits and pieces of you until it felt safe to be all of you again. As the feelings return, a shiver runs down your spine. This is your gift in this life—feeling things so deeply. You vibrate with emotional wisdom beyond this dimension.

You are the one who holds the cosmic language of the galaxy—you've danced with each archetype, collecting a bit of each one of us, to become whole yourself. You've merged and become one with us all. For your own sake. For your own sanity. Until you couldn't tell where you ended and another began. You've pinched a bit of wisdom off each one of us, tucked it under your wing, to become the wisest, the most all-knowing, whimsical creature that's ever graced Earth.

You are the Holy Ghost. You are the empty air taking form—the one who whispers past our shoulder and moves our hair when nothing and no one is around. You are a soul adrift, moving from this world to the nearest star and back again. You're as tender as a moonbeam, delicately brushing our lips with your ghostly kiss.

You long for that which can never be, a story of unrequited love. Your longings are as deep as the ocean from which you came and to which you will return. Secrets kept in a vault at the river's bottom. We hand them to you because we know we can trust you with those mysteries. They will never see the light of day. You guard them as you do our hearts, with the purity of unconditional love and valor.

You speak without words. You've always spoken silently. And yet, you're the loudest voice in our hearts. You smell of Angel's breath and cirrus clouds. You shake the stars from your hair as you land earthside just for a bit—until the Angels tug at your curls once more, wanting you for their own, as we all do. So off you float, into the world where you feel most at home.

"Stay," we whisper. But as your lips brush ours and your breath sighs into our hair, you say, "I'll see you in your dreams."

GRATITUDE

My two sons have been my greatest teachers of the archetypes.

My Taurus boy, Jonah, has shown me what a grounded, logical, kind, and gentle soul looks like—with a sprinkle of stubbornness and a determination unmatched by any other. His love for music and his ability to play any instrument, write music, and perform make my heart sing. Venus is loud in his chart, shining down from the top on all else. He has a magic touch with food and warms my belly with his homemade breads and meals.

My Aquarius boy, Elia, has taught me how to throw my well-laid plans out the window and show up for the unexpected in this lifetime. He's pushed me outside my comfort zone and shown me my strength. He gave me nineteen of his years. He's taught me how to be in a deep relationship with him now that he's across the veil and that our connection never dies—only the physical form. He told me, *"Face what you fear, and you'll become free."*

One day, as the stars aligned and magic was afoot, I met my most powerful mentor, guide, teacher, and friend, Debra Silverman. She cast her Gemini grin my way, and I followed her home into the classroom of the stars . . . literally! I sat through her astrology school, Applied Astrology, with rapt attention, where I moved from student to teacher.

Debra captured me with her jokes, a Gemini's lightness of being, and a love so strong that only her Aries moon can take credit for. A Gemini teacher and a Sagittarius student—it was a classroom of laughter and wisdom, silliness, and unfiltered truths. She fed me her wisdom of the great beyond, and I ate every morsel on my plate. We couldn't keep a serious face if we tried. You can't take us anywhere—we get too excited and find ourselves in trouble when we're together. Imagine the delight when Sagittarius looks over at Gemini, and the mischievous grin is already dancing on Gemini's lips—it's a love story.

These tales might not exist if it weren't for my Capricorn beastie, Tara, cheerleading me on. I call her "Beastie on the Eastie" because she lives on the East Coast, and she refers to me as her "Bestie on the Westie" because I live on the West. What would I do without her? Upon writing these tales, I handed each one over to her. And in her true Capricorn way, she took each one into her hands—hands that never shook or wavered—and held them tenderly, with great care. I lean into her, and she stands firm. On the days I get stuck or question my writing, she shows up, sitting next to me, backbone straight and tall. She is my unwavering person of clear, strong wisdom. How one person can hold so much wisdom in one lifetime is beyond me. When my Sagittarius fires and Leo Rising get out of control, she shows up and provides a container. When I say, "I'm about to do this . . ." she shows up with logical reasoning. She has talked me down from the fence many times. She's my voice of reason. Her loving and strong hand has saved me time and again. My Tara. My beastie. My pillar. How I found such a friend in this world can only be part of a giant cosmic blessing. Her Libra moon loves to dance together with mine, as we do most things in conjunction. When something happens to her, she can't help but say it's happening to *us*. She moves me toward my Libra North Node. She emanates her Pisces Rising—it's the first thing you'll feel from her if you're ever so lucky to be in the same room as her. She is aqua blue in energy—floating and dancing her way around in mermaid spirit. She's a drink of water after being in the desert sun. You felt her in the Capricorn Tale as she brought it to life for me.

These are my people. These are where these tales were birthed from. They grabbed my hand, and I simply followed.

ABOUT THE AUTHOR

Malika Semper is a certified astrologer and intuitive counselor. She has been professionally practicing astrology since 2016. Her love for the cosmos started in her teen years, and she has been studying and using it in her life ever since.

As a writer and teacher, her most popular course is the *Synastry Series*, where she teaches relationship astrology—how one person can affect another—which she has taught hundreds of students over the years.

Malika has studied extensively with Debra Silverman and is a DSA-certified astrologer and Master Mentor for Debra's *Applied Astrology* program. She has also studied with astrologers such as Divine Harmony, Kelly Surtees, and Kira Sutherland, just to name a few.

Her greatest joys come from soul connection with others, being with her children, and sharing insights with people through the eyes of the stars.

She is a double Sagittarius (Sun and Moon) with a Leo Rising and a Stellium in the fourth house.

She lives in beautiful Oregon. When her head is not in the stars, she finds her peace in nature—hiking deeply into the forests surrounding her or swimming in the rivers and lakes to find refuge from the hot summers.

Usually with her head in a book or her pen answering crosswords, she's an introvert. She has fostered a deep connection with her sons and cultivated an inner circle of a few special souls who mean the world to her.

You might also find her in the kitchen, cooking or baking old German family recipes handed down from her mom and Oma Ernie. When all her Sagittarius gets activated, you'll hear her as she'll be the loudest laugh in the room. Is she laughing at her own jokes? Perhaps. Is she complaining about the heat of the Sun? Most likely. Her soul yearns for the frost and snow of winter, when there's a nip to the air and the world is much more quiet.

Learn more about Malika and her signature classes at:
https://malikasemperastrology.com

Connect with Malika:
Instagram: @malika_semper_astrology
FaceBook: Malika Semper Astrology
YouTube: Malika Semper Astrology